Henry Ford

Read These Other
Ferguson Career Biographies

Maya Angelou
Author and
Documentary Filmmaker
by Lucia Raatma

Leonard Bernstein
Composer and Conductor
by Jean F. Blashfield

Shirley Temple Black
Actor and Diplomat
by Jean F. Blashfield

George Bush
Business Executive
and U.S. President
by Robert Green

Bill Gates
Computer Programmer
and Entrepreneur
by Lucia Raatma

John Glenn
Astronaut and U.S. Senator
by Robert Green

Martin Luther King Jr.
Minister and
Civil Rights Activist
by Brendan January

Charles Lindbergh
Pilot
by Lucia Raatma

Sandra Day O'Connor
Lawyer and
Supreme Court Justice
by Jean Kinney Williams

Wilma Rudolph
Athlete and Educator
by Alice K. Flanagan

FERGUSON
CAREER BIOGRAPHIES

Henry
Ford

Industrialist

BY MICHAEL BURGAN

Ferguson Publishing Company
Chicago, Illinois

An Editorial Directions Book

Library of Congress Cataloging-in-Publication Data
Burgan, Michael.
    Henry Ford / by Michael Burgan.
    p. cm. — (A Ferguson career biography)
    ISBN 0-89434-369-6
    1. Ford, Henry, 1863–1947—Juvenile literature. 2. Automobile industry and trade—
United States—Biography—Juvenile literature. 3. Industrialists—United States—Biogra-
phy—Juvenile literature. 4. Automobile engineers—United States—Biography—Juvenile
literature. [1. Ford, Henry, 1863–1947. 2. Industrial. 3. Automobile industry and trade—
Biography.] I. Title. II. Ferguson career biographies.
TL140.F6 B87 2001
338.7'6292'092—dc21
[B]   00-049499

Copyright © 2001 by Ferguson Publishing Company
Published and distributed by
Ferguson Publishing Company
200 West Jackson Boulevard, Suite 700
Chicago, Illinois 60606
www.fergpubco.com

Printed in the United States of America
Y-3

CONTENTS

Henry Ford

Henry Ford at age two and a half. Even as a young boy, he was very good with tools and machines.

A MECHANICAL MIND

During the Civil War (1861–1865), many farmers saw a rise in demand for their crops. One such farmer was William Ford of what is now Dearborn, Michigan. To increase his productivity, Ford bought a reaper—a machine used to harvest grain. This mechanized farm tool was drawn by horses. And these animals were also an important part of America's transportation network. But within half a century, horses were an increasingly rare sight on many roads, thanks largely to William Ford's oldest son.

Henry Ford was born on July 30, 1863, in what is now Dearborn, Michigan. Growing up on his father's farm, Henry thought people worked too hard planting and harvesting crops. He saw machinery as the best way to reduce this labor.

From an early age, Henry surrounded himself with tools and constantly tinkered with them. William Ford encouraged his son's curiosity, and Henry responded creatively. He repaired handles on tools, made metal hinges, and fixed wagons. In one early display of his skill, he invented a system that allowed a wagon driver to open a gate without leaving his seat. Later in his life, Henry wrote, "My mother always said I was a born mechanic."

Working the land. In the mid-1800s, many farmers used horse-drawn threshers on their farms.

Mary and William Ford. Henry's parents always encouraged their son's curiosity.

When he was about ten years old, Henry and some classmates built their own mill. First they built a dam across a small brook that carried runoff water from a nearby field. Then, using a small water-wheel, a coffee grinder, and a rake, the boys created a mill that ground up potatoes, clay, and pebbles.

Henry's early mechanical experiences were not always completely successful, however. In one experiment, Henry built a simple steam engine. To create steam power, water is boiled by burning either wood or coal. The steam produced then moves the engine's piston. Unfortunately, Henry's apparatus exploded, and a piece of metal pierced his lip. Another bit of flying debris hit a boy in the stomach. In addition, the fire that followed the explosion burned down part of the schoolyard fence. However, when William Ford heard of the fire, he did not punish his son. He simply warned Henry to be more careful when he "played."

An Important Year

In 1876, two events pulled Henry farther into the world of machinery and engineering. The first occurred right before Henry's thirteenth birthday. He and his father were in a wagon traveling to Detroit when a self-powered vehicle came rumbling up the road. Henry had never seen anything like it. Steam engines like this were used to power threshers and saws, and they were usually pulled by horses from one place to another. But this "road engine" used its own power to move the cart that it sat on. An engineer stood behind the steam boiler, feeding it coal and steering the contraption.

Henry asked his father to stop the wagon. Then he leaped down to chat with the engineer. The man's name was Fred Reden, and he explained how the vehicle worked. Over the next year, Henry often

A steam-powered carriage. Young Henry was excited by the new uses for steam engines.

met with Reden, who let him feed coal into the boiler and run the engine. Henry had been introduced to a passion that would dominate his life. His goal, he said, was "making a machine that would travel the roads."

Later that year, Henry had an engineering triumph of his own. For years, he had been trying to repair broken watches. He spent time taking them apart and exploring their workings. Finally, he succeeded in putting a watch together so that it kept time. In the years that followed, this self-taught watch repairman could fix almost any timepiece, using only crude, handmade tools. Sometimes Henry walked into Detroit to find spare parts. His quest for new mechanical opportunities brought Henry to the big city over and over again.

Apprenticeship

When he was sixteen, Henry headed to Detroit for his first real job. His father was not happy though. Mr. Ford wanted his son to be a farmer, like him. But Henry knew his future lay with machines, and he took a job at the Michigan Car Company. At its sprawling factory in the city, the company made railroad cars. Henry lasted just six days at that plant, and he does not mention this job in his autobiography, *My Life and Work*. But during this short stint, Henry undoubtedly saw the simple assembly line used there to manufacture cars.

In Henry's day, most young men who wanted to learn a trade started off as apprentices. The "students" worked side by side with master craftsmen to learn their skills. Henry's real apprenticeship began at the James Flowers and Brothers Machine Shop. The Flowers brothers, who knew the Ford family, used an assortment of machines to make brass and iron products. Henry later wrote that this kind of training was ideal for any young mechanic. "Machines are to a mechanic what books are to a writer. He gets ideas from them, and if he has any brains he will apply those ideas." Throughout his early training, Henry stockpiled the ideas that would shape his future.

While working at the Flowers' shop, Henry earned extra money repairing watches. He also found time to read American and British magazines on science and mechanics. Some of the articles talked about an engine powered by gasoline—the internal combustion engine. A German engineer named Nikolaus Otto had invented one of these gas engines in 1876. For the time being, however, Henry was more interested in steam engines. Nevertheless, the internal combustion engine always stirred his curiosity.

In the summer of 1880, Ford went home to Dearborn to help his father with the harvest. Afterward, he returned to Detroit and took an apprenticeship at the Detroit Drydock Company, the largest shipbuilder in Detroit. The company made steam engines of all sizes, and Henry learned the details of their operation. He also continued to repair watches; he even thought about making and selling his own

Workers at the Detroit Drydock Company. Henry Ford was an employee there in 1880.

watches. His idea was to make "a good serviceable watch" for about 30 cents and then sell it in huge quantities. But after deciding that not enough people would want his watches, Henry abandoned the idea.

The Horseless Carriage

In 1882, Henry completed his apprenticeship at Detroit Drydock. He was now a full-fledged machinist and an expert in steam engines. He went back to the family farm. His father might have thought Henry was finally ready to settle into agriculture, but Henry still had machines on his mind. He became a representative for the Westinghouse Company. This company made steam-powered road engines like the one he had seen when he was a boy. Henry repaired and ran the engines for farmers in southern Michigan.

For a few years, Henry worked with the road engines. On the farm, he puttered in his workshop. He thought about building a steam-powered "horse-less carriage" that could be driven on roads. At that time, many engineers and inventors were toying with this idea, and some were already making progress. But first Henry concentrated on bringing mechanized transportation to the farm, with a steam-powered tractor. Henry thought machines could do farmwork faster and more cheaply than horses.

Over time, however, Henry decided a steam engine was too big—and too risky—for the kind of vehicle he envisioned. The boiler could explode, just as his childhood steam engine had. In 1885, Henry did some repair work on an Otto gas engine. The internal combustion engine, he began to realize, might be a more practical power source for a horse-less vehicle.

For the next few years, whatever engines Henry built or tested stayed in his shop. No one close to him ever reported seeing a working engine—steam- or gas-powered—that propelled a vehicle.

At age twenty-three, Henry Ford managed to run a farm while he pursued his mechanical interests.

FIRST ACHIEVEMENTS

Meanwhile, back on the Ford farm, Henry developed a new interest. Late in 1884, Henry went to a local dance. He spent some time with Clara Jane Bryant, a young woman he had recently met. Henry impressed her with a watch he had made. Afterward, Clara told her parents about Henry: "He's a thinking, sensible person—serious-minded." Clara and Henry's relationship quickly blossomed, and they were married in 1888.

A year or so before the wedding, William Ford made his son an offer. He was willing

Clara Jane Bryant. She and Henry Ford were married in 1888.

to give Henry 40 acres (16 hectares) of good timber land. By cutting and selling the wood, Henry would be able to afford married life. But his father's offer had a catch: He expected Henry to eventually farm the land and give up his career as a machinist. Henry took the land, accepting his father's terms, as he later wrote, "in a provisional way." His long-term goal was still to build a workshop and continue experimenting with engines.

Once he was settled on his land, Henry cut timber and processed wood. He also continued to repair engines, as well as work on his own. In 1890, he began working on a two-cylinder gas engine that he hoped would power a bicycle. Modern bikes had been perfected only a few years earlier, and cycle manufacturing was progressing rapidly in the United States. The technology for making bikes was often applied to the development of horseless carriages. Henry quickly saw, however, that his gas engine was too heavy to power a bicycle.

More Experiments in Detroit

Around this time, Ford took a job as an engineer and machinist for the Edison Illuminating Company, which generated electricity for Detroit. The timber on his land was all cut, and Ford was finished with farm life. He also knew that he needed to learn more about electricity, which would play a part in powering any horseless carriage he built. Clara Ford was reluctant to leave the farm, but she trusted her husband's talents. So the Fords moved to Detroit in September 1891.

Employees at the Edison Illuminating Company. For a time, Ford worked for this electric company.

At first, Ford worked the night shift at the Edison Company. Once he switched to days, he spent all his free time experimenting in his small workshop. "I cannot say it was hard work," Ford wrote in his autobiography. "No work with interest is ever hard."

Finally, on December 24, 1893, Ford was ready to test his own gas engine. The flywheel, which was used to turn the piston, had come from an old lathe. The piston itself was homemade, and Ford had used scrap metal for other key components.

As Clara Ford prepared the next day's Christmas feast, Ford brought the engine into the kitchen. Their newborn son, Edsel, slept in the next room. Ford needed his wife's help to make the engine run. She fed the intake valve with gasoline while Ford

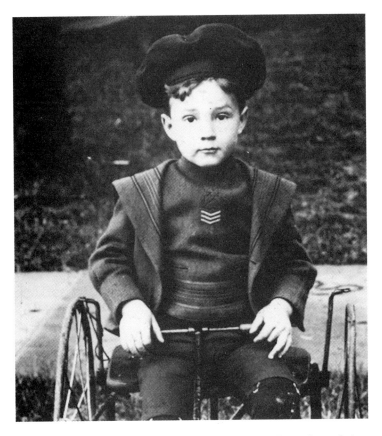

Edsel Ford in 1898. This young boy went on to play a big role in his father's life.

turned the flywheel. Air and gas filled the cylinder. To ignite the explosion that powered the piston, Ford created a spark using the house's electrical current. As he did, the kitchen light dimmed. As crude as the engine was, it roared to life and ran for several minutes. "I didn't stop to play with it," Ford later said. He was ready to build a more refined two-cylinder engine.

Competition and Cooperation

During the late 1880s and early 1890s, many machinists and engineers around the world were working with the internal combustion engine and trying to create "motor carriages." Two of the biggest breakthroughs came in Germany. In 1885, Gottlieb Daimler received a patent for the first motorcycle, which was powered by a gas engine. About the same time, Karl Benz was perfecting a motorized tricycle, which has been called the first gas-powered "car." Other inventors were using steam and electricity (from batteries) to power crude automobiles.

In the United States, brothers Frank and Charles Duryea built the first American gas-powered car. They tested their vehicle in Springfield, Massachusetts, in September 1893. Steam-driven carriages had been on U.S. roads even earlier. By then, perhaps dozens of American inventors were devoting their energies to building horseless carriages. Most of them were unaware of developments made by others. In his autobiography, Ford wrote, "I had to work from the ground up . . . I could not know what [other inventors] were doing."

But shortly after his kitchen experiment, Ford met another automotive inventor—Charles B. King. Trained as an engineer, King designed several innovations for railroad cars. This work gave him the money to experiment with gas engines and horseless carriages. Based in Detroit, King designed and tested a four-wheeled car. After Ford became friendly with King, he learned even more about engines and auto design. When King tested his first car, Ford rode behind on his bicycle. Ford had never before seen a gas-powered carriage in action. Soon he would drive his own horseless carriage down the streets of Detroit.

The Quadricycle

Through 1895 and into 1896, Ford's vehicle took shape. After working all day for the Edison Company, Ford spent his nights in the workshop behind his

Gottlieb Daimler (left) and Karl Benz (right). These engineers made major breakthroughs with gas-powered engines.

Charles Duryea in Springfield, Massachusetts. In 1893, he invented the first gas-powered car.

house. He also enlisted talented craftsmen to help him. When relatives came to visit, Clara Ford explained her husband's absence by saying, "Henry is making something, and maybe someday I'll tell you."

Ford called his first automobile a "Quadricycle." It had four bicycle wheels with rubber tires and an iron carriage. Its engine had two cylinders and could produce about four horsepower. The driver sat above the engine on a bicycle seat. The Quadricycle had two forward speeds, but no reverse. Its top speed was about 20 miles (32 kilometers) per hour. Much of the car was made of wood. Unlike most horseless carriages of the time, however, the Quadricycle was small and light, weighing only 500 pounds (227 kilograms).

Early on the morning of June 4, 1896, Ford prepared to take his car on the road. But he had a small problem: The Quadricycle was too big to fit through the door of his workshop. Without hesitating, Ford took an ax and knocked down part of the brick wall. He then wheeled his car into the rainy darkness. After starting the engine, Ford climbed onto the seat, grabbed the steering rod, and set off. The first test of his own horseless carriage was underway. An assistant, Jim Bishop, rode just ahead of him on a bicycle.

Ford and his quadricycle. This vehicle had four bicycle wheels and a gasoline engine.

If any horse-drawn carriages were out so early, Bishop would warn the drivers of the motorized vehicle heading their way.

Ford took the car down a small alley and out into the street. After traveling only a short distance, the car stopped. Ford and Bishop found a problem with the ignition system. A few curious people gathered around, and Bishop later recalled that the people wondered "who was crazy enough to spend a lot of time and money on such a contraption." After a quick repair, Ford triumphantly finished his test drive.

Although the Quadricycle worked, Ford was not completely satisfied. He strengthened the car with more metal parts and added a cooling system for the engine. He also put in a bigger seat, so that he could ride with a passenger. Clara and Edsel sometimes accompanied him on trips into the country. Ford also spent a lot of time on the streets of Detroit, and he attracted many onlookers. "If I stopped my machine anywhere in town," he wrote, "a crowd was around it before I could start up again."

An Inspiration

A few months after his first drive, Ford went to a convention held in New York by the Edison Company. At the convention, Ford met the man the company was named for—Thomas Alva Edison. Edison gave America electric lights and the phonograph, among other creations, and he was the country's most respected inventor. Edison was curious about Ford and his horseless carriage. Ford demonstrated some of his car's features as he explained them to Edison. The great inventor struck the table. "Young man," he said, "that's the thing! You have it. . . . Keep at it." Edison's enthusiasm stirred Ford's determination to keep improving his car. Years later, Ford and Edison grew to be close friends.

Back in Detroit, Ford soon became a businessman as well as an engineer. He sold his improved Quadricycle for $200. Already, Ford wanted to do more than merely make a few cars in his spare time. "I was looking ahead to production," he later wrote, "but before that could come I had to have something to produce."

Ford started designing a new model. Along the way, some local investors agreed to back his efforts. The investors, however, were impatient with Ford, who always wanted to experiment and improve his work. So this business arrangement did not last.

By 1899, Ford had finally built what he consid-

Ford with Thomas Alva Edison. Edison was an important inventor who offered support for Ford's ideas.

ered to be a successful motorcar. He began looking for new investors to help him manufacture the car. On August 15, 1899, Ford left his job at the Edison Company. Making cars was no longer a hobby for Ford; now it was his career.

Detroit Automobile Company, around 1900. Ford served as the company's chief engineer.

THE BUSINESS
OF CARS

In August 1899, the Detroit Automobile Company opened for business, with Ford as its chief engineer. He did not invest his own money in the company, but he agreed to give his investors the rights to his automotive patents. The company's first model, a delivery wagon, went on sale early in 1900.

In its ads, the Detroit Automobile Company touted the wagon's quality, assuring that it would run for at least fifteen years. In a test drive, the local post office used the wagon for a mail delivery. The motorized vehicle completed the rounds in one-fourth of the time it took a horse-drawn carriage. After another test run, a Detroit journalist wrote that the wagon was "swifter than a racehorse; it flew over the city streets."

But Ford and his company had problems. The shop could not produce vehicles as quickly as it hoped. At one time, the company said it would make eight different models, but its total production was low. Workers assembled the cars by hand, and parts had to be checked and adjusted to ensure a proper fit. Other carmakers used techniques that seemed to produce more reliable cars.

While Ford wanted to improve his cars, his investors wanted a profit. This situation frustrated the talented young man. Ford wrote in his autobiography, "I found that the new company was not a vehicle for realizing my ideas, but merely a money-making concern—that did not make much money." By the end of 1900, the Detroit Automobile Company was out of business.

Despite this setback, Ford was soon ready to try again. This time he would take a new approach. If he couldn't build reliable, affordable cars, he would build fast ones instead.

Racing to Fame

Almost as soon as engineers started building horse-less carriages, a daring group of drivers wanted to see how fast they could drive these new machines. Racing was also a way to create excitement about cars, which most people then considered just a noisy toy for the wealthy. Ford had not planned to race his cars, and he later felt the push for speed was bad for the automotive business. He wrote, "The attention of the makers was diverted to making fast rather than good cars." But Ford realized he had to take part in the racing craze if he wanted to demonstrate his engineering skills.

Ford improved his two-cylinder engine and mounted it on a simple chassis. In tests with his assistant Oliver Barthel, Ford managed to reach about 70 miles (113 km) per hour. When Detroit's first-ever car races were held, Ford's speed machine was ready to run.

On October 10, 1901, the city seemed to be taken over by automobiles. A parade of more than 100 cars—steamers, electrics, and gas powered—wound through the streets. The races were held at a track just outside town. The main event was a 25-mile (40-km) race. One of the competitors was Alexander

Ford and Oliver Barthel with the first Ford racer. This machine won a Detroit car race in 1901.

Winton, at that time America's champion racer. Winton was a bicycle manufacturer who had turned to making autos. He had recently set a record for the fastest mile, and his car's engine produced 40 horsepower—almost twice as much as Ford's racing engine. Winton was clearly the favorite to win.

The first races of the day took so long to complete that the main race was cut down to 10 miles (16 km). By now, some of the top drivers had dropped out of the race. Only two drivers rolled up to the starting line—Winton and Ford. Winton, with his powerful car and racing experience, quickly took the lead. But on the sixth lap, Ford began to close the gap. The crowd cheered for the local favorite. Then a cloud of blue smoke drifted up from Winton's engine, and a mechanical problem forced him to slow down.

As Ford shot ahead of the champion, the crowd went wild. In the stands, Clara Ford saw one man throw his hat on the ground and stomp on it with excitement. A woman jumped out of her seat and screamed, "I'd bet $50 on Ford if I had it." Ford kept the lead, winning his first race.

In the stands that day were some of the investors from the old Detroit Automobile Company. Impressed with Ford's success, the investors soon decided to back another car company. By the end of the year, Ford was chief engineer for the Henry Ford Company.

On His Own

Again, Ford and his investors did not agree on the company's direction. The investors soon brought in another engineer to look at Ford's methods, and he dismissed Ford's trial-and-error style. In March 1902,

Ford left the company and went out on his own. The Henry Ford Company continued to make cars—but under the name of Cadillac.

Ford now wanted to focus his attention on racing. He swore that his first race as a driver was his last, but he would continue to build racers for others to drive. He teamed up with Tom Cooper, a well-known bicycle racer in Detroit. Cooper wanted to race Ford's cars. The two men also enlisted another driver, Barney Oldfield. Soon Ford and his team had two race cars, the "Arrow" and "999," both named after famous railroad locomotives of the era.

On October 25, 1902, Oldfield drove "999" in its first race. Compared to Ford's earlier cars, this racer was a monster: nearly 10 feet (3 meters) long, it had a four-cylinder engine that produced about 70 horsepower. Ford later wrote, "The roar of those cylinders alone was enough to half kill a man." On the track that day, Oldfield won easily, setting a new American speed record for a 5-mile (8-km) race. Ford was pleased. He had proved once again that he could design and build a fast car. His reputation as an engineer was solid in Detroit, which was already becoming a leading automotive center. Once again, Ford was ready to go into full-time auto production.

An easy winner. Barney Oldfield drove the "999" racer in an October 1902 speed competition.

The Ford Motor Company

Even before the October victory with "999," Ford was preparing to build another passenger car. In August, Ford found a new financial backer: Alexander Malcomson, a local coal dealer. Working with Malcomson was Ford's business adviser, James Couzens, who had important managerial skills. Ford also teamed up with C. Harold Wills, a new shop assistant who played a large role in Ford's subsequent success. According to Allen Nevins, a biographer of Ford, "[I]n the design of all the company models of the next dozen years, it is impossible to disentangle Ford's work from that of Wills."

To build the engine for his new car, Ford hired two of the best machinists in Detroit, brothers John and Horace Dodge. Their shop was known for its skillful employees. Ford and Malcomson turned to other suppliers for automobile bodies, tires, and wheels. The major parts for each car cost about $370. Ford could sell the car at a reasonable price and still make a profit.

In June 1903, Ford was ready to assemble his new car. He, Malcomson, and their other investors officially formed a new company: the Ford Motor Company. Ford and Malcomson each owned 25.5 percent of the company's stock; other shareholders included Couzens and the Dodge brothers. Ford was in charge of design and manufacturing, while Couzens ran the office.

The first car sold was the Model A. Going back to his old concern about a vehicle's weight, Ford said the car "was lighter than any other . . . that had yet been made. It would have been lighter if I had known how to make it so." The basic model cost $850; a car with a rear seat cost $100 more. The company took out newspaper ads saying that the car was "specially designed for everyday wear and tear . . . a machine which will be admired by man, woman, and child alike for its compactness, its simplicity, its safety, its all-around convenience and—last but not least—its exceedingly reasonable price. . . ."

The first Model A sold in July 1903. Within nine months, the Ford Motor Company sold 658 cars, making a profit of almost $100,000. "The business went along almost as by magic," Ford wrote in his autobiography. His cars "were tough, they were simple, and they were well-made." Ford's company was not America's largest automaker, but it was successful. Still, almost from the first, a legal cloud hung over Ford's head, threatening to hamper his growing business.

Henry Ford in 1904. He joined other men in forming the Ford Motor Company the year before.

STRUGGLES AND SUCCESS

Years before Henry Ford built his first gas engine, George Selden applied for a patent for a gas-powered horseless carriage. Selden was an inventor and a lawyer. He spent years changing his application and finally received a patent for a "road locomotive" in 1895. Selden's car was not especially different from other motorized carriages that appeared before and after his. But his car had a combination of features, including a gas engine, that Selden claimed made his vehicle unique.

In 1899, Selden sold his patent to the Electric Vehicle Company. As its name suggests, the company planned to build electric cars, but gas-powered vehicles were emerging as the preferred type of horseless carriage. The Electric Vehicle Company decided it could make more money by exercising its legal rights as the owner of the Selden patent. The company did not build Selden's car; instead, it demanded a fee from any company that built gas-powered vehicles.

Rather than challenge this arrangement, many

The first factory of the Ford Motor Company. Over the years, the company experienced many ups and downs.

leading carmakers—including Ford's friend Alexander Winton—agreed to pay a royalty to the Electric Vehicle Company. But in return, the auto companies took control of the patent. In 1903, the companies formed the Association of Licensed Automotive Manufacturers (ALAM). The group soon had thirty members. Many small carmakers, such as Ford, did not join the group.

In July 1903, Ford saw a notice in a local paper. The ALAM announced that only ALAM members had the legal right to make or sell gas-powered cars. The notice warned that "any person making, selling, or using such machines made or sold by unlicensed manufacturers or importers will be liable to prosecution for infringement." Technically, Ford was breaking the law—and so were the satisfied customers driving his Model A.

Many engineers and inventors dismissed the Selden patent. One wrote, "[T]he engine shown in the patent was utterly impractical and a joke. . . . The claims were so broad that that they are ridiculous." Ford later noted that Selden's car was only an idea: "He had done nothing to put it into practice." The legal threat from the ALAM did not bother Ford. He said, "I believed that my engine had nothing whatsoever in common with what Selden had in mind."

Ford soon struck back. He printed his own notice, assuring his dealers and customers that the ALAM had no legal case and that his company would protect anyone prosecuted under the automakers' claim. Despite Ford's certainty about his position, in October 1903 the ALAM sued the Ford Motor Company. The suit, Ford realized, "was meant to scare us out of business." Ford was prepared to fight for his car and his independence.

Long Legal Battle

For almost seven years, the case against Ford and other auto companies dragged on in the courts. The ALAM had millions of dollars to spend on high-powered lawyers. Although he lacked that kind of money, Ford hired good lawyers of his own. The lawyers for both sides filed motions and gathered testimony, and the actual trial did not start until May 1909. On the stand, Ford admitted that he had borrowed from other inventors to develop his car. But so had Selden and others; no one had the right to claim a patent for an invention like the car. Ford said, "To teach that a comparatively few men are responsible for the greatest forward steps of mankind is the worst sort of nonsense."

When the trial ended, the judge found for the ALAM and the Selden patent. Ford and the other defendants had broken the law. The news shook Ford, but he wrote in a telegram the next day, "Selden suit decision has no effect on Ford policy— we will fight to a finish." Still, he was worried that customers might avoid his cars because they risked being sued—or even arrested. Ford even briefly considered selling his company to William Durant, head of General Motors. But Ford kept fighting.

The verdict for the Selden patent was appealed, and in November 1910, three judges heard the case. On January 9, 1911, they gave their unanimous decision: Ford and the other defendants had not infringed on the Selden patent. Selden's engine was not based on the Otto gas engine, the kind Ford and other carmakers used. The defendants, the judges said, "neither legally nor morally owe [Selden] anything."

Ford and his supporters rejoiced at the news. Ford later commented, "If we had not won the suit, there never could have been in this country such an automobile industry as exists." Others called Ford "the greatest man in the automobile world." With the patent case victory, Ford seemed like the biblical figure David, who killed the much larger and stronger Goliath. Actually, during the years of the trial, the Ford Motor Company had continued to prosper. Ford was on his way to building a great fortune. Much of that success rested on a new car.

Building the Ideal Car

Through the Selden case, Ford kept his automotive goals: Build a light, powerful, reliable, and affordable car. "I am going to democratize the automobile," Ford declared in 1909. By then he had already built the car that would achieve that goal. After releasing his first Model A in 1903, Ford produced new models, all with letters for names, all with improvements. The Model T, introduced in 1908, was the best of all.

The road to the Model T began in 1905. Ford learned of a superstrong yet light steel called vanadium. This steel, Ford realized, would help him build his "universal" car. Working with his top designers, Ford created the car with all the features he wanted. Most of these features had been tested in earlier models. Combined with the vanadium steel, Ford had his dream car.

Henry Ford: Industrialist

The 10 millionth Model T alongside the Quadricycle. Ford's inventions radically changed the lives of everyday people.

To Ford, "the important feature of the new model . . . was its simplicity." A simple car had fewer parts, so it was cheaper and easier to build. A simple car was also easy to fix. Instead of repairing broken parts, owners could replace them with new, inexpensive parts. Ford believed these parts "could be carried in hardware shops just as nails or bolts are carried."

Model T Hits the Road

When Ford took the Model T out for a test drive, he was thrilled with the result. One worker said Ford was "tickled to death" with his new car. The public liked it too. Drivers bought more than 10,000 Model Ts during the first year they were offered. These cars included different versions of the basic Model T. The sales for the Model T set a record for the Ford Motor Company. It now had more than 2,100 employees, and Ford prepared to build a new plant so that he could expand his operations.

In 1909, Ford stunned his shareholders with an announcement: The company would stop making other cars and build only Model Ts. Any new Ford car would have the same chassis. Ford also told his sales staff, "Any customer can have a car painted any color that he wants so long as it is black." Ford had a basic design that both he and his customers liked. Now he would focus his effort "on making the machinery to produce it, concentrating so completely on production that, as the volume goes up, it is certain to get cheaper per unit produced." In this way, Ford could keep his prices low, while guaranteeing his company's profits.

Ford believed his competitors thought he was crazy. They said his dream of a universal car would ruin the Ford Motor Company. But Ford was convinced he had built a car "for the great multitude." He declared, "No man making a good salary will be unable to own one—and enjoy with his family the blessing of hours of pleasure in God's great open spaces."

The Ford Motor Company assembly line. Henry Ford's ideas for assembling cars were innovative.

TWO REVOLUTIONS

5

For the next few years, the Ford Motor Company continued to grow. Ford's new factory opened in Highland Park, Michigan, in 1910. The company also built new plants around the United States. Parts for the Model T were shipped to these plants, where workers assembled the car. Next, Ford opened an overseas assembly plant near Manchester, England.

Fueling this growth was the increasing popularity of the Model T. After a brief price increase to pay for the new Highland Park plant, Ford lowered the price on his car. A

Model T that cost $950 in 1909 was only $490 in 1913. By then, 250,000 Model Ts were on the road. Part of the price reduction came after Ford achieved his goal of improving the manufacturing process for his car. In 1913, Ford introduced modern mass production to the industry.

The Birth of Mass Production

Henry Ford did not invent the car—he simply made it better and more affordable for more people. In the same way, the various elements that went into mass production existed before Ford. His genius was combining them in new and efficient ways.

Mass production relies on interchangeable parts. Before the Industrial Revolution of the late 1700s, craftsmen made parts for a piece of equipment, such as a rifle, by hand. The parts for one rifle differed slightly from another, even if they were made by the same person. Then Eli Whitney and other inventors began using machines to make parts that were identical—and interchangeable.

Another piece to the mass-production puzzle was first developed around the same time. Oliver Evans used steam-powered conveyor belts to move grain through his mill. This method helped shape the idea

The success of mass production. This represents one day's work in August 1913.

of the assembly line. Later, meatpackers used motorized belts to move cows and hogs through their processing plants. Ford specifically mentioned the packing plants as one of his inspirations.

Ford already used interchangeable parts. He saw the value of moving parts along a belt to bring them to the workers. Then he added another element—having each worker do just one specific job during the assembly process. Ford tested this new approach in April 1913. Mass production greatly reduced the time it took to assemble the parts of a car. For example, with the old method, it took one worker about twenty minutes to make a part called a flywheel magneto. Ford's assembly line reduced the time to five minutes.

In his autobiography, Ford outlined some of his principles for mass production. "A man shall never have to take more than one step, if it possibly can be avoided, and . . . no man need ever stoop over." Ford experimented with the height and speed of the assembly lines, trying to find the perfect arrangement. He also automated as much of the manufacturing process as possible. With mass production, Ford could make more cars with the same number of workers, letting him lower his prices.

Over time, other carmakers and other industries saw the benefits of mass production and adopted Ford's methods. No one questioned that the new method was good for business, but some wondered if it was good for workers.

Ford wrote that mass production reduced a worker's need to think, and he saw nothing wrong with that. He believed most workers wanted a job that required little thinking. Over time, however, some social critics said mass production turned workers into robots. Ford dismissed these "parlour experts," as he called them. Still, some workers later grumbled about the constant demands of the assembly line and nicknamed Ford "the speed-up king."

The Five-Dollar Wage

In January 1914, Ford announced another change that shook his competitors—and the rest of the world. From then on, almost all employees of the Ford Motor Company would make at least $5 per day, and the workday would be cut to eight hours. (Workers still had to put in a full day on Saturdays.) At the time, the average Ford worker earned less than $2.50 per day, and wages were even lower in other industries.

Once again, some people thought Ford was crazy. Other carmakers feared they would have to match Ford's raise or risk losing workers. The *Wall Street Journal* said Ford was bringing charity to business, where it did not belong. Others accused Ford of looking for publicity while trying to destroy his rivals. But most people—especially workers—welcomed Ford's bold move. To many Americans, Ford's success with the Model T and mass production made him a hero. The $5 wage added to that image.

To Ford, higher wages made perfect sense. He saw it as a social benefit that would give workers money to save and to spend. But he also saw the raise as good for the company. The higher wage would boost worker loyalty, which would increase productivity. He later wrote, "There was . . . no charity in any way involved. . . . We wanted to pay these wages so that the business would be on a lasting foundation. . . . A low wage business is always insecure." Ford could afford the raise: The company's profits were strong, and mass production promised to continue that trend. Ford saw the pay increase as a form of profit sharing that he paid up front, instead of waiting for the higher profits to actually come in. Higher wages also meant workers could afford to buy things—such as Ford cars. Other workers, in America and around the world, hoped that one day they might get raises too, and then they could also become Ford customers.

The Other Side of Better Pay

The announcement of the $5 wage drew thousands of people to Detroit, hoping to find work at the Ford

Motor Company. They filled the streets outside the Highland Park plant, even though the company said it was not hiring. Riots almost broke out, and the police used water hoses to control the crowd.

Meanwhile, Ford workers welcomed the higher wage. One employee told a reporter that his children could finally stop working and spend more time with their family. The Ford plant soon had a new nickname: "The House of Good Feeling." But the raise came with a cost: Ford now believed he had the right to control more of his workers' lives.

Ford in his Highland Park office in 1913. He took good care of his employees, but he also expected a lot in return.

The company set up a Sociological Department. Its goal was to help Ford workers with their education, health, and living conditions. Many of the workers were immigrants who spoke little or no English. Others were illiterate. The Sociological Department did indeed improve workers' lives, but the workers lost some of their freedom. Some people criticized Ford's direct involvement in his workers' affairs.

Ford later said he expected something from a worker in return for the higher wage: "The man and his home had to come up to certain levels of cleanliness and citizenship." And he admitted that at first the company went too far with its new role as a social helper. But Ford saw his help as a benefit for the workers, even if the workers did not always agree.

UPS AND DOWNS

6

By 1916, Henry Ford was the undisputed king of the automotive world. His company sold more than 700,000 Model Ts that year, and the car had now picked up the affectionate nickname of "Tin Lizzie." In the words of historian Samuel Eliot Morison, "The Model T was the car that revolutionized American life." Farmers added a special attachment to them and used the cars as pickup trucks. Workers could now live outside of cities and drive their Model Ts to work. Even in remote parts of the United States, people now had a new freedom of mobility, thanks to Ford's car.

The widespread use of the automobile also created new industries. Cars needed gas and repairs, so service stations sprang up. The drivers refueled their cars at roadside restaurants and then slept at inns overnight. Tourism grew, and tourists spent money at remote shops that hadn't existed before. This growth continued for decades to come. Perhaps Ford was only exaggerating slightly when he said, "I invented the modern age."

Ford had other interests beside cars. He renewed his interest in building farm tractors. As early as 1905, he experimented with building a gas-powered tractor. Over the years, Ford continued those efforts, and in 1915 he prepared to build a plant just for manufacturing tractors. Ford's projects—and his company—would keep expanding in the years to come.

But Ford saw himself as more than an engineer and a businessman. As his Sociological Department showed, Ford thought he could help end social problems as well. World War I (1914–1918) gave him the chance to act on those concerns.

The Peace Ship

World War I began in Europe in the summer of 1914. Many people thought this "war to end all wars" would be over in a few weeks, but the fighting dragged on. Some Americans supported Great Britain, whose main allies were France and Russia. Their major opponents were Germany and the Austro-Hungarian Empire. Ford, however, was one of the many Americans who opposed the war and any U.S. involvement in it. "I hate war," he said, "because war is murder, desolation, and destruction."

'Leading American pacifists asked Ford to help their efforts to end the war, and Ford agreed. His fame and money were powerful resources for the peace effort. In November 1915, Ford went to New York, his first stop on a trip designed to call for an end to the war. On November 24, Ford met with a group of reporters in a New York hotel.

"Well, boys," Ford said, "we've got the ship."

"What ship, Mr. Ford?" one journalist asked.

"Why, the *Oscar II.*"

The journalist was still in the dark. "What are you going to do with her?"

"Why, we're going to Europe to stop the war," Ford replied.

"Stop the *war?*"

Ford said with assuredness, "Yes, we're going to have the boys out of the trenches by Christmas."

Ford's ship was the *Oscar II*. He had chartered it from a leading steamship company, and the vessel was later dubbed the "Peace Ship." Ford then tried to recruit a number of prominent people to sail with him, including his old friend Thomas Edison and former president William Howard Taft. He failed to attract most of these famous figures. Still, even without celebrities, the peace mission created a buzz across America. Not all of it, however, was positive. Many newspapers called the voyage a "stunt." One New York paper called it "the cruelest joke of the century."

Clara Ford also opposed the trip, fearing for her husband's safety. German U-boats, or submarines, patrolled the Atlantic Ocean, and mines dotted the waters. Every week brought new reports of civilian ships going down because of the war. But Ford was determined to go.

The *Oscar II* sailed on December 4, 1915. The Atlantic crossing was rough, with storms and high seas, but the ship avoided any subs or mines. The *Oscar II* reached Oslo, Norway, on December 18. Ford had been sick for most of the voyage, and he stayed in Europe less than a week. The peace mission, however, went on without him, and he continued to sup-

The final launching of the Eagle boat. Ford thought that his ships could help end World War I.

port its efforts. Some of his former critics now had kind words for him. One paper that first attacked Ford now said, "Henry Ford deserves respect, not ridicule. No matter if he failed, at least he tried."

Once the United States entered the war in 1917, Ford supported the war effort. He wrote in his autobiography, "I believe that it is the duty of the man who opposed war to oppose going to war up until the time of its actual declaration." The Ford Motor Company built cars, trucks, and ambulances for the government. It also introduced the Eagle, a boat designed to hunt submarines. When World War I ended in November 1918, Ford and his company "went back to peace."

Legal War at Home

Around the time of the peace trip, trouble was brewing at the Ford Motor Company. In October 1915, James Couzens, Ford's trusted business manager, quit the company. He and Ford had begun to disagree on Couzens's role. Ford was eager to have more control over all of the company's operations.

By this time, Ford owned a majority of the company's shares. Other major shareholders included Horace and John Dodge. Since 1903, the Dodge brothers had supplied parts to the Ford Motor Company—and become rich from their Ford stock. In 1914, they stopped making parts for Ford and opened their own automotive company. The first Dodge car appeared the next year. Their dividends from the Ford stock had helped finance their venture. The Dodges' roles—as part-owners of the Ford Motor Company as well as competitors with it—soon created problems.

The Dodges did not like some of Ford's business

Horace Dodge. He and his brother owned Ford stock but went on to form their own car company.

decisions. They wanted Ford's guarantee that he would use his own money, not company profits, to build his tractor factory. Ford agreed. The Dodges also wanted Ford to pay higher dividends to all the shareholders. This time, Ford said no. He wanted to use the profits to build a huge manufacturing center on the River Rouge, outside of Detroit. The Dodges wanted the dividends so that they could expand their own car business. Ford's expansion plans would also lead to cheaper prices for the Model T, which would make it harder for the Dodges to compete. Ford's plans put the Dodge company at risk.

On November 2, 1916, the Dodges responded by suing Ford and his company. The brothers wanted the court to prevent Ford from using company funds for his expansion plans. The court soon agreed. The Dodges also wanted 75 percent of the Ford Motor Company's cash profits to be distributed to shareholders. Those funds equaled about $40 million.

As the lawyers prepared for trial, Ford gave interviews designed to win public support. He said his company was not interested in making "awful" profits, only reasonable ones. The Dodges' attorney, Elliott Stevenson, tried to use Ford's words against him in court.

"You say you do not think it is right to make such profits?" Stevenson asked. "What is this business being conducted for, and why is it being enlarged?"

"To do as much good as possible for everybody concerned," Ford replied.

The attorney prodded, "What do you mean by 'doing as much as good as possible'?"

"To make money and use it, give employment, and send out the car where people can use it."

Later Stevenson summed up Ford's position, not believing what he was hearing. "Your controlling feature, then, is to employ a great army of men at high wages, to reduce the selling price of your car, so that a lot of people can buy it at a cheap price, and give everybody a car that wants one?"

"If you give all that," Ford asserted, "the money will fall into your hands; you can't get out of it."

In Ford's earlier court battle—the Selden patent case—a group of manufactures tried to dictate how Ford made cars. The Dodge trial was also about control. Ford won the patent case, but this time he suffered a partial defeat. In 1919, the Ford Motor Company was ordered to pay a special dividend of about $19 million, with 10 percent of that going to the Dodges. But Ford was already planning a way to end further problems with his growingly disagreeable shareholders.

Edsel Ford. In 1918, he was elected president of the Ford Motor Company.

BUILDING AN INDUSTRIAL EMPIRE

At the end of 1918, before the final decision in the Dodge case was handed down, Henry Ford sent a letter to the board of directors of the Ford Motor Company. It contained his resignation as the president of the company. Ford told the board he wanted to pursue other interests. The board accepted Ford's resignation and elected his son, Edsel, as the new president. Henry Ford remained on the company's board of directors.

Business leaders and newspapers buzzed with the news, and everyone wondered what Ford would do next. The answer came in March 1919. A report in the *Los Angeles Examiner* described Ford's plan to start a new automobile company. "His idea," said the story, "is to make a better car than he now turns out and to market it at a lower price."

Ford said the Dodge trial had spurred this new plan. He wanted the control he lost when the court ordered the Ford Motor Company to pay out high dividends. Ford sought the freedom to reinvest in his company as he saw fit. He talked of designing an entirely new car and hiring up to 200,000 workers to build it.

There's no question Ford wanted total control over his own car company. But his intention to start a new company was most likely a ploy. The threat of a new Ford-built car competing with the Model T could hurt the Ford Motor Company. Its shares would become less desirable to any outside buyer and would lose their value. But they were extremely valuable to Ford. He soon began negotiating with the other shareholders to purchase their stock. The price wasn't cheap: Ford spent almost $106 million buying the 41.5 percent of the company he did not already own. He thought it was a small price to pay for what he wanted. On July 10, 1919, Ford became the sole owner of the company bearing his name, and he no longer needed to start another company.

Troubles Outside the Business

Never before had one American businessman owned such a valuable company. The various Ford plants were worth almost $1 billion. Ford could now expand his empire, investing millions at the new plant, called River Rouge or simply "the Rouge." But events outside the automotive business did not always go so well for Ford.

In 1918, the Democratic Party had asked Ford to run for the U.S. Senate in Michigan. Ford had supported the policies of President Woodrow Wilson, a Democrat. Ford lost a close race, and he spent almost two years trying to overturn the results with a recount. The effort failed. (Ford briefly considered entering politics again in 1922, as a presidential candidate, but changed his mind.)

During the time of his takeover of the Ford Motor Company, Ford was involved in a third lawsuit. This time Ford himself, not his business practices, were on trial. In 1916, the *Chicago Tribune* had called Ford "an ignorant idealist" for his antiwar efforts. Ford

Vote for
HENRY FORD
For Senator

The Workingman's Friend

Candidate for the U.S. Senate. Henry Ford campaigned to be senator but lost in a close race.

sued the newspaper for libel, and the case dragged on for years. In 1919, Ford once again faced attorney Elliott Stevenson in court. Stevenson did his best to show that Ford truly was ignorant.

Under Stevenson's questioning, Ford said he thought the American revolution began in 1812, not 1775. He did not know other historical information commonly taught in school. Finally Ford said, "I admit I am ignorant about most things." In the end, the jury agreed Ford had been libeled, but it awarded him just 6 cents in damages. Many average Americans supported Ford as he withstood Stevenson's bullying tactics. But one magazine saw the public display of Ford's ignorance as "pitiful." No one would ever deny Ford's engineering and business genius, but his public image was weakened.

Ford's reputation took another blow during the 1920s. In 1918, Ford had bought his own newspaper, the *Dearborn Independent*. He used it to promote his ideas and his cars. He felt he needed his own paper to combat the untruths told about him and about American society in other newspapers. Ford did not write the paper, though each issue had a column that reflected his views.

Starting in 1920, Ford and the paper ran into

The Ford International Weekly
THE DEARBORN INDEPENDENT

$1.50   Dearborn, Michigan, August 6, 1921   Ten Cents

And Now Leprosy
Is Yielding to Science
Years of experimenting brings a remedy

Fountain Lake, the
Home of John Muir
A story of naturalist's wilderness abode

Fighting the Devil in Modern Babylon
First of a series of articles on New York by Rev. Dr. John Roach Straton

Jewish Jazz—Moron Music—Becomes
Our National Music
Story of "Popular Song" Control in the United States

The Chief Justices of the Supreme Court
Only ten men have held this post since the tribunal was first organized

Teaching the Deaf to
Hear With Their Eyes
How Chicago is educating afflicted children

Many By-Products
From Sweet Potatoes
Recent discoveries prove great possibilities

The Dearborn Independent. *Ford owned this paper during the 1920s and wrote columns for it as well.*

trouble when some of its stories showed a bias against Jews. Ford did not have a personal dislike of all Jewish people. But he seemed to accept the stereotype of Jewish bankers supposedly controlling much of the world economy. The *Independent*'s stance was also influenced by the anti-Semitism—hatred of Jews—of some of Ford's associates. The paper's charges against Jews led to another lawsuit, and in 1927 Ford had to publicly apologize for the anti-Jewish writings. Shortly after, the *Independent* closed for good. This episode further stained Ford's image among some Americans.

Back to Business

Despite his political loss and legal troubles, Ford kept expanding his business. The company faced a difficult stretch in 1920 and 1921, when the American economy slowed and fewer people bought cars. Ford fired thousands of employees. He also found ways to cut his costs. Phones and other office items were eliminated. So were forms and efforts to collect statistics. This information was interesting, Ford said, "but statistics will not construct automobiles—so out they went." Within three months, the company quadrupled its cash on hand to $87 million and was back on solid ground.

In 1922, Ford expanded his car business with the purchase of the Lincoln Motor Company. At first Ford merely owned Lincoln; he let the previous owners run the company. Soon, however, Edsel Ford was in charge of Lincoln, which made luxury cars much different from the Model T. Henry Ford said about the Lincoln, "The man who makes it cannot buy it."

The Model T was still the preferred car for the average driver. During the early 1920s, the Model T was the world's best-selling car. In 1923, the Ford Motor Company sold almost 1.7 million of the car's different versions. The huge company producing these cars was more than just an automaker. Over the years, Ford bought other companies that helped him control all parts of his business.

In 1920, Ford bought land for his new Michigan Iron, Land and Lumber Company. He built sawmills to cut the lumber and kilns to dry wood. He also bought iron and coal mines. Ford built his own hydroelectric plants to power various small factories. In 1921, he became president of the Detroit, Toledo and Ironton Railroad, which ran alongside his River Rouge plant. He already owned a small fleet of barges and other ships that carried material across the Great Lakes.

Ford's car business also brought him into the world of wireless communication. He saw wireless telegraphs and radios as a way to communicate between the various parts of his growing empire. By 1928, Ford had what some newspapers called one of the largest wireless telegraphy stations in the world. In May 1922, Ford opened a commercial radio station, WWI. Ford employees with musical talents often played on the station's programs. The radio also broadcast nationally known performers and talks on social and scientific issues. Ford thought of starting the Ford Communications Company, but he disliked federal laws governing the operation of radio stations. He gave up both the wireless telegraphy and radio by the end of the decade.

Ford's ventures stretched overseas as well. In 1927, he bought land in the Amazon Valley of Brazil for his own rubber and lumber plantation. He built a small community for his workers called Fordlandia. Ford hoped the business there would help ease the poverty of the region, as well as benefit his company. Ford also opened automotive-assembly plants in Canada, Europe, South America, and Australia.

The Rouge

The greatest single piece of the Ford empire was the River Rouge plant. Back in 1915, Ford had identified a tract of land along the river as the perfect spot for a "superplant." (Ford also built his home, Fair Lane, farther along the river.) The trial with the Dodges delayed construction at the site, but Ford built his Eagle boats there during World War I. Automotive operations began there after the war.

Ford wanted the plant to be self-contained. He envisioned a place where he could turn raw materi-

Fair Lane. The Fords built this home near the River Rouge plant.

als into parts and parts into cars. Ships brought lumber, coke, and ore up the river. The plant's huge blast furnace produced iron for the Model T and Ford tractors. Ford also opened his own steel mill on the site. A foundry took raw metal and turned it into finished parts of iron, brass, and steel. These parts then went to Ford assembly plants around the world.

By 1927, the Rouge complex included ninety-three buildings on 2,000 acres (810 ha). More than 90 miles (145 km) of railroad tracks crisscrossed the property, and 27 miles (43 km) of conveyors moved parts through the buildings. Ford designed the plant in such a way that it was well lit and workers had to move as little as possible to do their jobs. In September, the final car-assembly line at the old Highland Park plant was moved to the Rouge, where 75,000 workers kept the plant humming. By then, the Ford Motor Company had a new car to produce.

The River Rouge plant in 1927. The complex had ninety-three buildings and 75,000 workers.

CHANGING
TIMES

By May 26, 1927, 15 million Model Ts had rolled off the assembly line at Highland Park. Two days before, the Ford Motor Company had announced it would stop producing the world's most famous car and introduce a new model. Ford, the man who had so drastically changed America, was not very open to change himself. It took years for him to decide to replace the Model T.

During 1925, profits at the Ford Motor Company had fallen. People were still buying the Model T, but more were turning to

Ford's competition. In his drive to build a cheap, reliable auto, Ford had not paid much attention to his car's appearance. The Model T was still a simple, boxy carriage on wheels. Buyers, however, now wanted cars with more style and comfort.

Edsel Ford tried to convince his father it was time to for a new model. So did Ernest Kanzler, who was Edsel's brother-in-law and a Ford Motor Company executive. In a memo to Henry Ford, Kanzler wrote, "We . . . have barely held our own, whereas competition has made great strides . . . our best dealers are low in morale and not making the money they used to."

Ford reacted angrily. In public he either ignored Kanzler or ridiculed him, and his relations with his son also became strained. Ford believed it was wrong for a car company to make new models all the time and then use advertising to convince the public they should get rid of their old cars. "We never make an improvement that renders any previous model obsolete," Ford wrote in 1922. Finally, however, Ford accepted that the Model T had to go.

The New Model A

Once the announcement was made, the American public waited anxiously to see if Ford could top the

Model T. Henry Ford and his son worked together to design the new car, which would keep some of the qualities of the Model T. Ford still wanted a reliable car. He also used his old methods, preferring to build and test designs and parts, rather than planning everything out in great detail.

When the car was complete, Ford took it for a test drive in a field. He returned and said, "Rides too hard. Put on hydraulic shock absorbers." Soon after, the Model A was ready for sale.

Henry and Edsel Ford with a Model A. This new car became the best-selling automobile in the United States.

The new Ford car had a top speed of 65 miles (105 km) per hour—more than 20 miles (32 km) per hour faster than the Model T. It also had improvements for safety and comfort, including shock absorbers, safety glass, and better brakes. Ford had achieved his goal of building a light, reliable, affordable car, while matching his competitors' features. On December 1, 1927, when the car was introduced to the public, 100,000 people jammed showrooms in New York City alone. Within a few weeks, about 500,000 Americans put down cash deposits to buy the new Model A.

In 1928, the company sold more than 630,000 Model As. The next year, the Model A was the best-selling car in America, with more than one and a half million cars sold. But 1929 was not a good year for the American economy. The stock market crash of October marked the end of a decade of prosperity. The country was about to enter the Great Depression, and the Ford Motor Company shared in the tough times.

Fighting the Depression

Before the end of 1929, Ford reacted boldly to the oncoming downturn. He announced price cuts and raised the pay for his workers to $7 a day (they had received an earlier raise to $6 a day in 1919). "The higher the wage," Ford explained, "the greater the purchasing power and the wider the variety of work that is set in motion." The raise did not last, however; by 1931, the country was deep into the Depression, and Ford cut back wages. By 1932, they fell to $4 a day. Ford also laid off about half of his workers and at times had to shut down the assembly line.

The Depression, however, did not end Ford's efforts to build better cars. At the end of 1929, Ford decided to build an engine with eight cylinders for the Model A. The more cylinders an engine has, the more power it can produce. Ford's competitors were introducing a six-cylinder engine, so he wanted to beat them with eight. The design of this engine had two sets of four cylinders placed at an angle forming a "V," so the engine was called a V-8.

These V-8 engines were not new, but no one had tried to build one for inexpensive cars. Ford was convinced he could. It took almost three years, but in March 1932 Ford introduced a Model A with the new V-8 engine. The car's basic model cost $460, and it received a good reception from the public. "I've got back my old determination," Ford told reporters, even though he was almost seventy years old and the company was going through tough times.

The engine needed some improvements, but the Ford Motor Company used the basic design of the V-8 for more than twenty years. The more powerful Model A was a favorite getaway car for gangsters, who appreciated its speed. John Dillinger, who was known as "Public Enemy Number One," wrote Ford: "You have a wonderful car. It's a treat to drive one."

Not everyone, however, was as happy with Ford and his company. The Depression led to massive unemployment, hunger, and homelessness. Some Americans lost their life savings, either from the stock market crash or the collapse of the banks that followed. Some people began to wonder if the whole capitalist system was about to fall. Some radical groups, such as the Communist Party, hoped it would.

The Communists found more Americans willing to listen to their message—that private industry hurt the working classes and that the government should run the economy. Others, who were not so radical, did not want capitalism to end; they merely wanted to form labor unions. The unions sought better pay and working conditions for the people lucky enough to have a job.

Violence at the Rouge

During the Depression, Henry Ford was still one of the most powerful capitalists in America. His company became a target for some of the frustrations of the day. On March 7, 1932, about 3,000 protesters, mostly Communists, marched on the River Rouge plant. They demanded a shorter workday, free health care, and the right to form unions. The Dearborn police turned on the crowd, which did not have a permit to march. The police fired tear gas, then attacked the protesters with their clubs. The Communists fought back with rocks or any other weapons they could find. Ford's security force also joined in, spraying the crowd with fire hoses. Then shots rang out, and police gunfire killed four protesters.

Ford had once been a hero to working people everywhere. He offered hope of better pay and working conditions. But his image soured after the 1932 "hunger march," and his relations with labor were strained. After the march, 15,000 people attended the funeral of the four dead protesters. Some in the crowd were Ford employees, and soon after the funeral they lost their jobs. They suspected fellow workers, called "spotters," had revealed their sympathy for the protesters.

Ford's spotters appeared to be typical assembly workers. In reality, they were spies for the company. The spotters reported on workers who wasted time or otherwise violated company rules. During the 1930s, the spotters reported on fellow workers who talked about forming unions or criticized Ford.

Ford did not like unions or any government effort to control his business. About government interference he said, "I was always under the impression that to manage a business properly you ought to know something about it." Under President Franklin Roosevelt, the government created an agency that encouraged companies within an industry to follow a code. The code spelled out wages and hours for workers. Ford refused to sign the code for automakers. The codes were declared unconstitutional by the Supreme Court in 1935. But the same year, Congress gave U.S. workers the legal right to join unions.

The United Autoworkers Union (UAW) formed the next year. Walter Reuther, a former Ford employee, was the UAW's chief organizer in Detroit. Ford and the other major auto companies tried to prevent the UAW from recruiting members. The autoworkers started holding sit-down strikes: They came to work, then sat down and refused to leave the plant. In 1937, General Motors and Chrysler reached agreements with the UAW, but Ford still held out.

On May 26, 1937, Reuther and other union organizers began handing out UAW pamphlets outside the Rouge plant. Ford's own security force stalked over and beat up Reuther and three other men, then dumped their bloody bodies down a steel staircase. The attack drew outcries in the press.

Ford thought popular opinion was against the UAW's efforts to unionize his plant. "Our workers won't stand for it, the public won't stand for it," he told Edsel. But the law was on the workers' side. In 1941, after a long court battle, the UAW and the Ford Motor Company reached an agreement. Ford still thought his workers would choose not to unionize, but only 2.7 percent voted against it. A close business associate later wrote that the union vote was "perhaps the greatest disappointment [Ford] had in all his business experience."

Clara and Henry Ford at Fair Lane in 1939. In their later years, the enjoyed the time they spent at their home.

A NEW ERA

During the years of labor difficulties, the Ford Motor Company also had other problems. Profits in 1937 fell drastically from the year before, and Chevrolet and Chrysler offered fierce competition. Ford had personal concerns as well. In 1938, at the age of seventy-five, he suffered a small stroke. Ford was still in charge of the company, although his son Edsel served as president. But Ford paid a little more attention to outside concerns.

Ford still had an interest in agriculture. He was trying to make paints and plastic from soybeans. He also wanted to set up "village industries." Since 1919, Ford had built small factories near farms, so farmers could make parts for his company and also work their land. Ford was also active with Greenfield Village, his "living museum" dedicated to American history.

By the end of the decade, another war was brewing in Europe. Adolf Hitler, the leader of Nazi Germany, wanted to expand his country's borders. Ford was sometimes seen as pro-German, or at least anti-war. After Hitler's troops invaded Poland in September 1939, some Americans thought the United States should not aid France and Great Britain, who were fighting the Nazis. Ford agreed, saying, "If we start shipping [arms] over there, we'll be in the war right away."

The next year, however, more Americans were ready to prepare for war, and Ford joined the effort. He built a factory called Willow Run to produce bomber planes for the U.S. military. The company had briefly built civilian planes during the 1920s and early 1930s.

The Willow Run factory was a huge complex. More than 1/2 mile (0.8 km) long, it held 70,000 workers. When famed pilot Charles Lindbergh saw the plant, he called it "a sort of Grand Canyon of the mechanized world." Workers began making B-24 bombers there in May 1942, five months after the Japanese attacked Pearl Harbor, Hawaii. Once the Unites States entered World War II (1939–1945), its industries quickly turned to making weapons and supplies for the military. The Ford Motor Company was soon one of the major contractors for the government.

Wartime Troubles

Production at Willow Run began slowly. The U.S. Army wanted 405 planes a month, but at first the actual number was much lower. When the plant was finally up to full speed in 1944, it easily met the Army's goal. During that time, other Ford plants were aiding the war effort. The company built trucks, jeeps, and gliders as well as engines for other airplanes.

While the plants operated around the clock, Ford suffered both a personal and business loss. His son, Edsel, died in May 1943. He had always had the difficult job of handling his father's whims. When Ford broke a business agreement or made a strange decision, Edsel was the one who had to deal with the outside world. Over the years, Ford had never let Edsel develop into a strong leader. But many people,

Ford at Willow Run. This factory produced bomber planes for the United States during World War II.

including President Roosevelt, found Edsel much easier to get along with than his father was. Inside and outside the business, people wondered who would run the Ford Motor Company—and what would be Henry Ford's role.

Behind the scenes, one of Ford's trusted assistants made a bid for power. Harry Bennett had run Ford's security department and handled any distasteful tasks. "I am Mr. Ford's personal man," Bennett once said. Bennett also seemed to have Ford's support to take over as president. But after Edsel's death, a new Ford emerged to take control—Henry Ford II.

Henry II was Edsel Ford's oldest son. Henry Ford was not particularly close to the grandson who shared his name, and he did not want Henry II in the company. Just twenty-five years old, Henry II

Another generation. Henry Ford II became president of the Ford Motor Company in 1945.

got permission to leave the U.S. Navy to join the family business. Slowly, with his mother and grandmother's support, Henry II gained power within the company. Henry Ford served as president immediately after Edsel's death, but as his health failed, he agreed to step down. Reluctantly, he let Henry II take over. The transfer of power came in September 1945, just a few weeks after the end of the war.

Henry II wanted to restore morale at the company, which had slipped since Edsel's death. The younger Ford immediately fired Bennett and his associates. He also hired new management to strengthen business. Shortly after Henry II took over, the Ford Motor Company was losing millions of dollars a month. The new executives, sometimes called the Whiz Kids, helped turn the company around. Early in 1947, Ford showed growing respect for his grandson.

The End of the Line

By then, Ford had some days when he was forgetful or acted oddly. He had suffered a second stroke in 1941. At times he would withdraw from other people, but on other days, his mind was still sharp. April 7, 1947, was one of Ford's good days. He went out for a drive to inspect damage caused by heavy rains the day before. Back at Fair Lane that evening, he followed his usual routine. But later that night, Ford had trouble sleeping. Clara came into his room and found him coughing. She ordered a servant to call for a doctor. By the time the doctor arrived, Henry Ford was dead. He has suffered a cerebral hemorrhage—bleeding in the brain.

A few days later, about 100,000 people came to Greenfield Village to pay their respects to Ford. America had lost one of its greatest innovators—and a very complicated man. Ford's refusal to compromise helped build his empire. It also almost killed his business when consumers' tastes changed. Ford brought Americans into the modern age, yet he cherished the past. He was a genius at industrial production and engineering, but he was ignorant in other ways. Ford wanted to help others, but he could be cruel to his own son. He violently opposed unions, yet when he finally accepted them he was more generous than other business leaders. He largely opposed charity and instead promoted "self-help." But his wealth helped start the Ford Foundation, one of the richest charitable organizations in America.

Paying respects. Henry Ford's funeral was attended by thousands of people.

Ford was much more than an automaker, but the Model T—a simple, sturdy car—made his reputation. As a newspaper wrote at the time of Ford's death, he put "in the reach of the greatest number of people a useful product which would lift the whole level of living. . . ." With all his faults, Ford was seen as a hero in his day. At the least, he changed the world in ways few other individuals ever have.

TIMELINE

1863   Henry Ford born on July 30 in what is now Dearborn, Michigan.

1879   Works in Detroit machine shops

1888   Marries Clara Jane Bryant and settles in Dearborn

1891   Returns to Detroit and begins working at the Edison Illuminating Company

1893   Becomes a father with the birth of his only child, Edsel; tests his own internal combustion engine on December 24

1896   Tests his first car, the Quadricycle, on June 4

1899   Becomes a partner in the Detroit Automobile Company

1901   Starts the Henry Ford Company, which remains in business less than a year; on October 10, wins his first automobile race

1903   Forms the Ford Motor Company with a small group of investors; sells first Model A

1908	Introduces the Model T
1911	In January, wins his appeal of the Selden patent case
1913	Uses first automotive assembly line at his Highland Park plant
1914	Announces a wage of $5 per day for most Ford Motor Company employees
1915	Sails on December 4 for Europe on the Oscar II—the "Peace Ship"
1918	Loses race for U.S. Senate
1919	Loses lawsuit brought by Horace and John Dodge and pays out large dividends; takes complete control of the Ford Motor Company on July 10
1927	Opens full production of the River Rouge plant; ends production of the Model T and introduces new Model A
1932	Produces a V-8 engine for the Model A; has problems outside the Rouge during a hunger march
1937	Tries to keep unions out of his plants
1941	Signs an agreement with the United Autoworkers Union
1943	Resumes presidency of the Ford Motor Company after the death of his son, Edsel
1945	Steps down as president of Ford Motor Company; is replaced by grandson Henry Ford II
1947	Dies at age eighty-three on April 7

HOW TO BECOME AN ENTREPRENEUR

The Job

Have you ever baby-sat neighborhood kids? Mowed a lawn or two in the summer? Then you already know something about being an entrepreneur. You've set your own hours, named your prices, and raked in the dough. Or something like that. The entrepreneurial spirit has long been strong in kids and teens; this is evident in the number of junior achievement organizations, such as Future Business Leaders of America (FBLA), devoted to the interests of young entrepreneurs. A Gallup poll found that 70 percent of high school seniors want to own their own businesses someday.

Though entrepreneurial enterprises have long been popular with teenagers, people often outgrow the ambition to embark on their own businesses. If you start a small business while still living at home, you have a bit less to lose—you don't have a family to support, a life-long savings to wipe out, or rent due. But many adults ignore the risks of entrepreneurship. Some of the biggest corporations of today started out as small businesses: Coca-Cola was a concoction by a Georgian pharmacist who jugged his mixture in his backyard, then carried it to Jacob's Pharmacy to sell for a nickel a glass. And it seems there are even more entrepreneurial success stories today. Dineh Mohager invented Hard Candy cosmetics by mixing nail polishes together, gave the colors mock-exploitative names like Scam and Skitzo, and made gross sales of more than $10 million her first year of business. Dave Kapell invented Magnetic Poetry and now pulls in $6 million a year in sales.

But you don't have to invent a new fashion trend or popular novelty to strike out on your own. Though the numbers vary from study to study, the American Association of Home-Based Businesses (AAHBB) reports that there are more than 24 million home-based businesses in the United States. Some of these businesses may be making big money, but most are simply making their founders comfortable. In addition to providing services and making good living wages, many small business owners are fulfilling their dreams. For example, a personal chef may find the slower pace of creating individualized menus much more satisfying than the odd hours and frantic demands of a restaurant kitchen. A husband and wife may gladly quit their full-time jobs to open up their home as a bed-and-breakfast.

Owning a small business has been part of the American dream since the earliest days of the country, and the late twentieth century saw a great increase in entrepreneurial ambition. This may be in part because of the downsizing trends of American companies. Whereas earlier in the twentieth century, a person could work for one company until retirement, such job security has become more rare. It's increasingly common for men and women in their fifties to lose their jobs, and find themselves with few job prospects. With severance pay in hand, these people often invest in the businesses they've been longing for, recognizing these ventures as no more risky than any other career pursuit. Once upon a time, a person chose a job path and stuck with it; these days, people experiment with a variety of careers throughout their lives.

There are more than 400 colleges and universities that offer entrepreneurship courses—200 more than there were in 1984. There are also more organizations, periodicals, and Web pages advising people on how to start their own businesses and keep them running. *Entrepreneur* and *Success* magazines publish special issues devoted to small business and maintain Websites. The Edward Lowe Foundation gives small business owners access to extensive databases, research, and conferences and publishes *Entrepreneurial Edge* magazine. The Small Business Administration (SBA) guarantees more than $10 billion in loans every year; 24 percent of the loans from the SBA's largest program go to minority-owned businesses. The SBA also provides business start-up kits, workshops, and research assistance.

This wealth of information, along with the ease of accessing it via the Internet, has undoubtedly played a part in the boom in small business. Technology in general has made it easier to run your own business from home. Computer software, specially designed for your profession, takes much of the time and effort away from administrative details. E-mail and fax allows you better communication, and the Internet puts you in touch with market research, industry support, and ways to better promote your business.

Structure

While there are a lot of resources to help you get your business started, there are also a lot of things you have to figure out about yourself first. Do you have the personal characteristics necessary for running a successful business? You'll need self-motivation for making contacts, pursuing clients and projects, and getting the work done—you won't have a supervisor giving you deadlines and checking your work. You'll also need dedication; it may be easy in the early days of the business to give up when the going gets rough, but you have to keep in mind that a new business can take a few years to get off the ground. Self-confidence is also important, because you'll be marketing yourself and your talents. And because the work may not be steady, you must be good at budgeting money for the lean months.

Once you've decided that you're up to the task of small business ownership, you'll need to consider the pros and cons of entrepreneurship. Depending on the nature of your business, you'll have the freedom to set your own hours, keep your own schedule, and possibly work at home. But you'll only get paid when you're actually doing work—you won't get vacation pay or sick leave. You also won't get company health benefits or a retirement plan. The success of your business will be based mostly on your own efforts—this can be both a plus and a minus. While you can take full credit for your success, you also must do all the work yourself. If you are working for a company, there are receptionists to answer the phones, accountants to handle the finances, and advertising departments to promote the company, while you can focus on your own assignments. But with your own business, you may have to take responsibility for every aspect of its operation, from finding clients to billing them. You also need to keep in mind that about one-half of all small businesses fail. You may want to explore a college entrepreneurship program. Many business schools are offering courses in entrepreneurship; these courses, and whole entrepreneurship programs, have gained a great deal of popularity in the last ten years. Often these courses are led by people who have started their own successful businesses.

Still ready for self-employment? First, you'll need to choose what your business will be. You may want to work in a field already familiar to you, a business in which you'll be able to use your talents and professional contacts. You'll definitely want to choose something you're interested in. But some people embark on businesses they know little about—those who have the money to invest in successful franchises like McDonald's or Dairy Queen may only be interested in the big profits promised by the franchisers. But, if you're like most people, you'll be starting your business on a shoestring and expanding later.

After you've decided on your business, you'll begin to do research. You'll contact professional organizations, chambers of commerce, the SBA, and other organizations to learn about the industry and marketplace. You'll read industry reports and magazine articles, visit Websites, maybe even attend trade shows and conferences. You'll interview other entrepreneurs. You'll also find out what licenses and certification you'll need to obtain. In the research stage, you may learn that there's not enough money to be made, or that there are too many similar businesses in your area, or that there's not much of a future in the field. Or you may find out that there's great demand for such a business and that there's a lot of small business support within the industry. If your research is encouraging, you'll start to develop your new business. This may be as simple as investing in some software and making some calls. But, in most cases, it will be much more intensive. Experts recommend a business plan, which involves defining your business, setting goals, and predicting income. Not only will the business plan be needed in getting loans, but it will help you keep your plans in focus. It will also help you determine what equipment and staffing you'll need. The American Home Business Association (AHBA) and the SBA are a few of the organizations that can help you develop a business plan.

"Niche" marketing is an important aspect of any business's success. What will set your business apart from others? How will you attract customers to the unique qualities of your product or service? This is where your originality and imagination come in. Figuring out what makes your business special, determining its niche, will help you promote your business and secure loans and other financial backing.

Now we're at the tricky part—where's your initial investment money going to come from? Even if you don't need much equipment and promotion to get started, you'll need money in the bank for operating expenses, including your own salary. Before starting your business, make sure you have enough money to get by for at least the first year. Some people get started with their own savings or with severance pay from former employers. A few others have spouses who work full-time and can provide additional security. Many develop their own businesses part-time, while still employed. Some get loans from a bank, the SBA, or a commercial finance company. But others simply leap in, without money or plans, hoping to solicit enough business to pay the bills for a while.

Despite all the careful planning and research advised by business experts, there are many people who stumble onto their own entrepreneurial success. Dineh Mohager, the founder of Hard Candy, was a medical student when she sold her first bottle of nail polish to a local department store. Dave Kapell was a musician and songwriter when he invented Magnetic Poetry. No matter whether you just jump into the world of self-employment or you map out a detailed business plan, some very important elements for every small business owner are good luck and great timing, factors difficult to depend upon.

Outlook

Despite some discouraging statistics that put small business failure at 50 percent, the number of entrepreneurial ventures will only increase. The majority of business school graduates will make their careers with entrepreneurships, either by starting their own businesses or by hiring on with small business owners. With a number of professional organizations and the SBA devoted to small business, the new entrepreneur can find a great deal of support—technical, financial, and emotional.

TO LEARN MORE ABOUT ENTREPRENEURS

Books

Bernstein, Daryl. *Better Than a Lemonade Stand: Small Business Ideas for Kids.* Hillsborough, Ore.: Beyond Words, 1992.

Erlbach, Arlene. *The Kids' Business Book.* Minneapolis: Lerner, 1998.

Greenberg, Keith Elliot. *Bowerman and Knight: Building the Nike Empire.* Woodbridge, Conn.: Blackbirch Press, 1997.

Haskins, Jim. *African American Entrepreneurs.* Black Star Series. New York: Wiley, 1998.

Merrill, Jean. *The Toothpaste Millionaire.* New York: Houghton Miffin, 1999.

Nelson, Sharlene. *William Boeing: Builder of Planes.* Danbury, Conn.: Children's Press, 1999.

Older, Jules. *Anita!: The Woman behind the Body Shop.* Watertown, Mass.: Charlesbridge, 1998.

Websites
EntrepreneurMag.com
http://www.entrepreneurmag.com
Articles and tools for the entrepreneur

Forum for Women Entrepreneurs
http://www.fwe.org
A group that supports and promotes entrepreneurship for women in technology and health care businesses

Where to Write
American Association of Home-Based Businesses
P.O. Box 10023
Rockville, MD 20849
To learn about membership support and other benefits

Edward Lowe Foundation
58220 Decatur Road, P.O. Box 8
Cassopolis, MI 49031-0008
For information about small business resources

National Association of Women Business Owners
1411 K Street
Washington, DC 20005
national@nawbo.org
To learn about membership for women entrepreneurs

U.S. Small Business Administration
409 3rd Street, S.W.
Washington DC 20416
For small business statistics and other relevant information

HOW TO BECOME A BUSINESS MANAGER

The Job

All types of businesses have managers, including food, clothing, banking, education, health-care, and business services. Managers make policies and carry out the firm's operations. Some managers supervise an entire company or a geographical territory of a company's operations, such as a state. Other managers oversee a specific department, such as sales and marketing.

Business managers make sure the daily activities of a company or a department follow the company's overall plan. They set the organization's policies and goals. They may develop sales materials, analyze the department's budget, and hire, train, and supervise workers. Business managers often do the long-range planning for their company or department. This includes setting goals for the company and developing a plan for meeting those goals. A manager who is in charge of a single department might be asked to cooperate with other departments. A manager in charge of an entire company or organization usually works with the managers of various departments and oversees all departments.

If the business is privately owned, the owner may also be the manager. A large company, however, has a group of executives above the business manager.

Top executives, such as the *company president*, set the organization's goals and procedures. The chief executive officer, chief financial officer, chief information officer, executive vice presidents, and the board of directors assist them. Top executives plan future business goals and develop ways in which divisions and departments can work together to meet the company's goals. Sales and budgets are reviewed on a regular basis to check progress. The president also directs programs within the organization and sets aside the necessary funds. Dealing with the public is a big part of an executive's job. The president must deal with executives and leaders from other countries or organizations, and with customers, employees, and various special-interest groups.

Some companies have an *executive vice president*, who directs the activities of one or more departments, depending on the size of the company. In very large organizations, executive vice presidents may be highly specialized. For example, they may oversee the activities of business managers of marketing, sales promotion, purchasing, finance, personnel training, industrial relations, administrative services, data processing, property management, transportation, or legal services. In smaller organizations, an executive vice president might be responsible for several departments. Executive vice presidents also assist the president in setting and carrying out company policies and developing long-range goals. Executive vice presidents may serve as members of management committees on special projects.

Companies may also have a *chief financial officer* or CFO. In a small business, the CFO is usually responsible for managing money. This includes budgeting, capital expenditure planning, and cash flow, as well as financial reviews. In larger companies, the CFO may oversee financial-management departments. He or she will help help other managers develop financial and economic policies and carry them out.

Chief information officers, or CIOs, are in charge of their company's information technology. They determine how information technology can best be used to meet company goals. This may include researching, purchasing, and overseeing the set-up and use of technology systems, such as Intranet, Internet, and computer networks. These managers sometimes work on a company's Website too.

Managers of companies that have several different locations may be assigned to specific geographic areas. For example, a large company with stores all across the United States is likely to have a manager in charge of each "territory." There might be a Midwest manager, a Southwest manager, a Southeast manager, a Northeast manager, and a Northwest manager.

Requirements

High School   The educational background of business managers varies widely. Many have a bachelor's degree in liberal arts or business administration. If you are interested in becoming a business manager, you should start preparing in high school by taking college-preparatory classes. Because the ability to communicate is important, take as many English classes as possible. Speech classes are another way to improve these skills. Courses in mathematics, business, and computer science are also excellent choices to help you prepare for this career.

Postsecondary   Business managers often have a college degree in a subject that meets the needs of the department they direct. For example, a degree in accounting for a business manager of finance; a degree in computer science for a business manager of data processing; and a degree in engineering or science for a director of research and development. As computer usage grows, managers are often expected to have experience with the information technology that applies to their field.

Many managers have graduate or professional degrees. Managers in highly technical manufacturing and research activities often have a technical or scientific master's degree or a doctorate. A law degree is necessary for managers of corporate legal departments, and hospital managers generally have a master's degree in health services administration or business administration.

Exploring

To get experience as a manager, start with your own interests. Managerial talents are used in any organized activity, whether you're involved in drama, sports, the school paper, or a part-time job. Managerial tasks include planning, scheduling, supervising other workers or volunteers, fund-raising, or budgeting. Local businesses also have job opportunities that give you firsthand knowledge and experience in management. If you can't get an actual job, try to set up a meeting with a business manager to talk with him or her about this career.

Employers

In 1998, the United States had more than 3.3 million jobs for general managers and executives, according to the U.S. Bureau of Labor Statistics. While these jobs were found in every industry, 60 percent of them were in the wholesale, retail, and service industries. In a 1998 survey of members of the American Management Association, 42.6 percent of the 4,585 participants worked in manufacturing. Approximately 32 percent worked in the services industry, which includes banking, health care, and the tourist industry.

Virtually every business in the United States hires managers. Obviously, the larger the company, the more such jobs it is likely to have. Companies doing business in larger geographical territories are likely to have more managers than those with smaller territories.

Starting Out

Generally, students interested in management need a college degree, although many retail stores, grocery stores, and restaurants hire promising applicants who have only a high-school diploma. Job seekers usually apply directly to the manager of such places. In some industries, management applicants need at least a bachelor's degree—either in a field related to the industry or in business administration. Often, they also need a graduate degree. A degree in computer science is an advantage. Your college placement office is often the best place to start looking for a job. Listings can also be found in newspaper help-wanted ads.

Many companies have management-trainee programs that college graduates can enter. Such programs are advertised at college career fairs or through college job-placement services. Often, however, management-trainee positions in business and government are filled by employees who already work for the organization and who show the traits needed for management.

Advancement

Lower-level employees who show managerial traits, such as leadership, self-confidence, creativity, motivation, decisiveness, and flexibility, fill most business-management and top-executive positions. In small firms, advancement to a higher management position may come more slowly than in larger firms.

Taking part in educational programs available for managers may speed up advancement. These are often paid for by the organization. Company training programs broaden knowledge of company policy and operations. Also consider training programs given by industry and trade associations and continuing-education courses in colleges and universities. These can inform managers of the latest developments in management techniques. In recent years, large numbers of middle managers were laid off when companies streamlined operations. As a result, competition for jobs is keen, and a commitment to improving your knowledge of the field and related subjects—especially computer information systems—may help set you apart.

Business managers may advance to executive or administrative vice president. Vice presidents may advance to top corporate positions—president or chief executive officer. Presidents and chief executive officers, upon retirement, may become members of the board of directors of one or more firms. Some business managers go on to establish their own companies.

Work Environment

Business managers usually have comfortable offices near the departments they direct. Top executives may have large offices and enjoy such privileges as executive dining rooms, company cars, country-club memberships, and liberal expense accounts.

Managers often travel between national, regional, and local offices. Top executives may travel to meet with leaders of other corporations, both within the United States and overseas. Meetings sponsored by industries and associations take place regularly and provide good opportunities to meet with peers and keep up with the latest developments. Large corporations often transfer people between the parent company and their other local offices or subsidiaries.

Earnings

Salary levels for business managers vary, depending upon the employee's level of responsibility and length of service, as well as the type, size, and location of the organization. Top-level managers in large firms earn much more than their counterparts in small firms. Also, salaries in large metropolitan areas such as New York City are higher than those in smaller cities, and salaries in manufacturing and finance are higher than salaries in most state and local governments.

According to a 1998 survey by the American Management Association, the average base salary of U.S. managers was $92,700. Top executives of large corporations are the highest-paid management personnel. The average base salary for these managers is around $144,000. Lower-level managers might earn $55,000 to $60,000.

Benefits are usually excellent for business managers, and may even include bonuses, stocks, company-paid insurance premiums, company cars, country-club memberships, expense accounts, and retirement benefits.

Outlook

Employment of business managers is expected to grow at about the same rate as other occupations through the year 2008, according to the U.S. Bureau of Labor Statistics. Many openings arise when managers are promoted, retire, or leave their positions to start their own businesses. The salary and prestige of these positions make them highly desirable, and competition will be intense.

Projected employment growth varies by industry. For example, employment opportunities in management in the computer and data-processing fields should double, while employment in manufacturing industries is expected to decline. Growth in service industries is expected to be faster than average.

TO LEARN MORE ABOUT BUSINESS MANAGERS

Books

Erlbach, Arlene. *The Kids' Business Book.* Minneapolis: Lerner, 1998.

Haskins, Jim. *African American Entrepreneurs.* New York: Wiley, 1998.

Nelson, Sharlene. *William Boeing: Builder of Planes.* Danbury, Conn.: Children's Press, 1999.

Older, Jules. *Anita!: The Woman behind the Body Shop.* Watertown, Mass.: Charlesbridge, 1998.

Websites

American Management Association

http://www.amanet.org

For news about management trends, resources on career information and finding a job, and an on-line job bank

Association for Women in Management
http://www.womens.org/
An organization that provides information about careers for women in management

Junior Achievement
http://www.ja.org
For information about programs for students in kindergarten through high school

Where to Write
American Management Association
1601 Broadway
New York, New York 10019-7420
212/586-8100

Association for Women in Management
927 15th Street, N.W., Suite 1000
Washington, DC 20005
202/216-0775

Junior Achievement
One Education Way
Colorado Springs, CO 80906
719/636-2474

National Management Association
2210 Arbor Boulevard
Dayton, OH 45439-1580
937/294-0421

TO LEARN MORE ABOUT HENRY FORD

Books

Aird, Hazel B., and Catherine Ruddiman. *Henry Ford: Young Man with Ideas*. New York: Macmillan, 1984.

Gourley, Catherine, Henry Ford Museum and Greenfield Village. *Wheels of Time: a Biography of Henry Ford*. Brookfield, Conn.: Millbrook Press, 1997.

Harris, Jacqueline. *Henry Ford*. New York: Franklin Watts, 1984.

Middleton, Haydn. *Henry Ford*. New York: Oxford University Press, 1998.

Mitchell, Barbara. *We'll Race You, Henry: A Story about Henry Ford*. Minneapolis: Lerner, 1991.

Websites

Driving Force: Henry Ford

http://www.time.com/time/time100/builder/profile/ford.html
Time magazine's profile of Ford as one of the most important businessmen of the twentieth century

Henry Ford and the Model T
http://www.wiley.com/products/subject/business/forbes/ford.html
From a book on U.S. business leaders, highlights of Ford's accomplishments

The Life of Henry Ford
http://www.hfmgv.org/histories/hf/henry.html
A biography from the Henry Ford Museum

Model T Ford Club of America
http://www.mtfca.com
Information about the Model T for both collectors and the curious

A Science Odyssey: People and Discoveries: Henry Ford
http://www.pbs.org/wgbh/aso/databank/entries/btford.html
A biography with a link to a more detailed discussion of the assembly line

Interesting Places to Visit
Henry Ford Estate: Fair Lane
University of Michigan at Dearborn
4901 Evergreen Road
Dearborn, MI 48128-1491
313/593-5590

Henry Ford Museum and Greenfield Village
20900 Oakwood Boulevard
Dearborn, MI 48124-4088
313/271-1620

Jerome and Dorothy Lemelson Center for the Study of Invention and Innovation

National Museum of American History, Room 1016
Smithsonian Institution
Washington, DC 20560-0604
202/357-1593

National Automobile Museum

10 Lake Street South
Reno, Nevada 89501
775/333-9300

INDEX

Page numbers in *italics* indicate illustrations.

ABOUT THE AUTHOR

Michael Burgan is a freelance writer of books for children and adults. A history graduate of the University of Connecticut, he has written more than thirty fiction and non-fiction children's books for various publishers. For adult audiences, he has written news articles, essays, and plays. Michael Burgan is a recipient of an Edpress Award and belongs to the Society of Children's Book Writers and Illustrators.